Hymns and Spiritual Songs

The Use of Traditional and Modern in Worship

John Leach

Director, Anglican Renewal Ministries.
Formerly Vicar of St. James, Styvechale, Coventry

GROVE BOOKS LIMITED
RIDLEY HALL RD CAMBRIDGE CB3 9HU

Contents

Acknowledgements

As I launch my maiden Grove Book, a twenty-year-old ambition has been fulfilled. It is good to have the chance to write on something I feel passionately about. Grateful thanks are due to the Group for the Renewal of Worship (GROW) for welcoming me and providing such stimulating company, and to those who read and commented on this manuscript. Special thanks to David Poulter of Coventry Cathedral. I felt this booklet should be vetted by a real musician, and I am grateful for his advice and friendship. And I hope you like it too!

The Cover Illustration is by Peter Ashton

First Impression April 1995
Reprinted with corrections December 1999
ISSN 0144-1728
ISBN 1 85174 288 3

1
Introduction

Church growth expert Dr Eddie Gibbs has a favourite phrase which I have heard him use on several occasions: 'A large church is not a large small church.' In other words, if we pursue church growth we need to realize that our church will change into a completely different animal as it gets bigger. The whole nature of what we do and the way we do it will have to change; we cannot just carry on as before only more so.

It is my conviction that modern church music, particularly that coming from what may be labelled the 'Renewal' stream, is not modern traditional church music but a completely different phenomenon. Yet one sees in many churches new music being used as if it were the same as old music—songs being used as if they were hymns. This booklet is designed to help planners and leaders of worship, and musicians involved in playing for worship, to understand the difference.

Why? Not, I want to say loudly and clearly right at the start, because one sort is 'better' than another. It is not my intention to enter into this kind of competition at all. All I want to do is to help us to understand what a particular piece of music is intended to do, so that we can ask it to do that and not something else to which it may be unsuited. I do not believe a hammer is *intrinsically better* than a screwdriver, but it is better for nails. If we can understand what new music is designed to do, and how it is made to be used, we might save ourselves a lot of bother trying to make it do something for which it is clearly inappropriate.

Different bits of this booklet will be useful for different people. Some of it is fairly technical in the realms of music and electronics, and clergy may well be unfamiliar with those worlds. Other parts will be more concerned with theology and spirituality, and may bore your PA operators to tears. But my hope is that I have provided a resource for the local church which, when seen all together, will be useful. So I have tried to make even the technical sections readable. At least they do not go on for too long!

Renewal Music and Renewed Worship

The first thing to understand is that renewal music is a symptom of a much deeper renewal, which has led to a new and different understanding of what worship is. In a previous Grove booklet James Steven has provided us with a good account of the thinking behind Restorationist worship, and while Christians from the mainstream denominations would not go along wholeheartedly with all 'new church' thinking, they have clearly been influenced significantly by it.[1]

Some key elements here would include *immediacy, intimacy* and *involvement*. The Holy Spirit is present, and likely actually to do things to the worshippers, not least in this current 'Toronto' phase, from the context of which I write. We are present at worship to become intimately involved with God, to touch his heart and to expect him to touch ours, and we are present also to be active in worship, rather than simply to listen to someone (or ones) up the front doing it for us. If worship is supposed to be both a duty and a joy, renewal worship is about putting a bit more of the joy back in.[2] We will be coming back again and again to these three core values, and we will see that they dictate much renewal praxis.

But there are other factors at work rather than just the theological. A whole new musical technology has sprung up over the last thirty years which is now very readily accessible to musicians. This has affected the types and styles of music now being produced.

Renewal music also has a new definition of 'excellence.' It is often thought that music from, say, the choral tradition appropriately strives for excellence, whilst for the charismatics any old spur-of-the-moment stuff will do. This is no more true than it is to say that all church choirs are excellent. What has changed is the way excellence is defined. Since involvement is one of the core values of renewal worship, to be excellent it does not have to be clever, complicated, impressive or difficult; it has to be accessible. The most simple of tunes may lift the hearts of the worshippers to God, and yet be considered by musical purists to be worthless, rightly so in one sense. It depends, as we have said, on what you are trying to make it do.

And of course, like any other field of enterprise, renewal music has its own terminology and jargon, which can be intimidating to those not in the know. This factor too needs to be appreciated in trying to understand it. I will try not to use too much of it in this booklet, and to explain what I do use.

The 80/20 Rule

Although I am going to be drawing some distinctions between hymns and worship songs, it is clear that this will only be valid up to a point. So I will be trying to draw out trends which I believe are generally correct. The 80/20 rule says that while eighty percent of what one says is probably correct, twenty percent is likely to be incorrect—though you cannot tell which

---

1   J Steven, *Worship in the Restoration Movement* (Grove Worship Series No 110) (Nottingham: Grove Books, 1989)

2   It is not my intention here to argue about the merits of renewal worship, or to discuss whether it is actually a collection of individuals on some kind of an experience trip. No doubt any style of worship has a philosophy behind it which would work perfectly were it not for the fact that some of the worshippers are sinners! I'm simply wanting to be descriptive.

is which! This will allow you to have some fun trying to find the twenty per cent exceptions. Nevertheless it is my conviction that modern music is significantly different from traditional hymnody.

Some have gone to great lengths to try to distinguish what the author of Ephesians meant when he differentiated between psalms, hymns and spiritual songs (Eph 5.19). Personally I find this hermeneutically dangerous, and its results too tenuous to take seriously. Any such exercise is surely in danger of reading back into the New Testament twentieth century ecclesio-musical practice. But what I do want to do is to distinguish between some of the current manifestations of worship music. Whether or not there is any tie-up with New Testament worship I do not know. The point simply seems to be that a range of different types of music were, and presumably still are, appropriate.

2
What's The Difference?

I want to list twelve differences which exist (bearing in mind the 80/20 rule) between what we now call 'hymns' and 'worship songs' or 'choruses.' They fall roughly into two groups: those, firstly, which have to do with their musical style; and then those to do with their context in worship. The first section may, as I have mentioned, be a little technical for some, although I have tried to make it as simple as possible, and probably too simple for any real musicians who may have picked this book up by mistake. But press on; it gets easier!

Musical Differences
1. Different Roots
Traditional hymns come largely from a classical background. A quick glance at the composers' index of a hymn book will show the extent to which people like Bach, Clarke, Gibbons, Handel, Haydn, Holst, Mendelssohn, Parry, Purcell, Sullivan, Vaughan Williams and others are responsible for the music we use. Add to this the number of traditional folk tunes featured in most hymn books, and a clear picture emerges of a particular style of singing which comes out of what we may term 'classical music.' Even when more modern hymns are written they tend to use the form and style of these classical hymns, and even on occasions use new words sung to old tunes.[3] We will explore further the distinctive style of this kind of hymn writing, but we do need to understand that renewal music comes from a very different background, that of the Black Gospel tradition which in turn led to blues, jazz, rock-'n'-roll and pop music. These very different ancestries have enormous implications for the performance and use of church music.

2. Different Musical Style
Let's get technical for a moment. It is possible to break music down into its three elements, and to see how each of these has been fashionable for different periods of church history. *Melody* is the first, the tune or air of the piece; then comes *harmony*, the underlying chordal structure which ties the melody into a particular key and gives it shape and definition; and thirdly there is *rhythm*, which is about the way the music moves forward through time.

---

3 A read (or sing) through *100* and *More Hymns for Today* shows this clearly. as does an exploration of much of the modern evangelical hymnody from the Jubilate Group.

In the mediaeval church plainsong or plainchant gained wide acceptance. This was for unaccompanied voices, and it consisted only of melody. There was no harmony, or at the most (in some later developments) nothing but parallel fifths, and the rhythm was that of natural speech, with no measures or bars to keep it together.

Then harmony became the ruling factor, with the chordal structure underlying the melody gaining more and more prominence, to the point where it is easy in the worst cases to see the tune as simply being the set of notes which happen to make up the top line of the chords. This was the era of the hymn, and the reason why many of them are so unmemorable is that it is the harmony which is important, and it is harder to remember and sing a harmony than a melody. Obviously when used carefully melody and harmony can enhance each other, but sadly many hymns do not achieve this. The rhythm of hymns is almost exclusively minims and semi-breves (or crotchets and minims in up-to-date books!) which move along uniformly with a gap at the end of each line.

But we have now entered the era of the third element, and in renewal songs it is rhythm which is paramount. The tunes may be fatuous and the harmony may consist of one chord change per line up to a maximum of about three, but the rhythm drives the song and makes it a memorable and exciting experience for the worshippers.

3. Different Instrumentation

It is easy to see, continuing in this line of thinking, that different styles will work well with different instruments. A solo flute or violin will be excellent for the melody of a song, but will be unable to add effectively to the harmony on its own (unless it races about up and down arpeggios). Similarly a drum kit will be great for rhythm, but will not help the melody much. A pipe organ may be good for the melody and the harmony, but is difficult to play very rhythmically, not least because of the time-lag between hitting the key and hearing the sound. Thus as rhythm has become predominant in worship songs, the instrumentation has moved more and more away from the church organ and onto the guitar (which can provide rhythm and harmony) and piano (which is pretty good for all three). Since most modern songs are written from guitars or keyboards, it is easy to see why they sound less than their best on the organ, just as the reverse is true of classical music.

4. Different Use of Rhythm and Harmony

We have already noted that most hymns, written in classical style, are a selection of chords one after the other, with one chord (or more) per word. Take for example Bach's *Passion Chorale*. The chord sequence begins: A minor/F/C(first inversion)/D minor/C/D minor 7 (first inversion)/G/C, and

7

after that lot we have only reached the end of the first four words. Even if this notation means nothing to you, and you would not recognize a first inversion if one came and bit you on the leg, you will realize that there are a lot of chords for just one line. This is the classic hymn style, and it explains why hymns are not usually played on the guitar!

A half-way stage became popular in what might be termed the 'mission' hymns of the late nineteenth century. Here one chord would last for more than one syllable, so that, for example, the words 'What a friend we have in Jesus' would all be sung over just two chords, F and Bb. However, the rhythm would be pretty similar to the classic hymn style.

With modern songs the transition is complete, with the use of few chords to cover several words, and a much more varied rhythmic style. So Noel Richards' *Jubilee Song* has the words 'We have called on you Lord, and you have heard us' sung to just two chords, with a dotted and syncopated rhythm. Worship songs work with this use of harmony and rhythm, and must therefore be arranged instrumentally in a way which is appropriate.

5. Different Sorts of Rhythm and Harmony

Not only is the quantity of chords used different; so is their quality. Without getting too technical, there is in modern worship a much greater use of what classically-trained musicians would call discords rather than chords. A basic chord usually consists of a triad of the first, third and fifth notes of the scale. By tweaking them slightly changes can be made (from major to minor or diminished chords, for example), and by adding to them chords like dominant sevenths can be formed. You may not understand the terminology, but you would be able easily to recognize the difference if you heard them. But chords with more than four notes would be rare in most early classical music. The one significant exception to this rule is J S Bach, who regularly used chords of which any contemporary jazz player would be proud: this may explain his popularity with jazz musicians such as Jacques Loussier and the Swingle Singers, and rock players like Keith Emerson.

However, the rise of jazz and blues allowed musicians to experiment with extra notes which did not really belong in the chords, but which in their own way added atmosphere and, yes, beauty to more traditional chord structures. Rather like Impressionist paintings, they could be frowned upon for not obeying all the rules of what they *should* be like, but nevertheless created evocative atmospheres which, to those who like that sort of thing, were beautiful. Worship songs belong to this heritage, but many of their harmonic components are simply not in the vocabulary of some classically-trained church musicians, who might regard them as simply 'wrong' in the same way that Botticelli might have regarded Turner's painting as 'messy.'

Just as modern music breaks out of classical harmonies, so too it is very

8

varied in its rhythm. A good renewal repertoire might contain everything from hard rock to bossa nova, from swing to jazz waltz, and even Latin and reggae beats. Increasingly there is experimentation with the latest dance, rave and rap rhythms. Minims and semi-breves are things of the past!

6. Different Use of Improvisation

If there are problems about the chords and rhythm which are supposed to be played, things get even worse when you move on to music which is not supposed to be there at all, and so needs to be made up. Some church organists are proficient enough to be able to improvise if the hymn finishes early before the collection has reached the front, but much renewal music is written with the intention that most of it is to be created as you go along. Improvisation is something to be used not just after the song, but during it as well. Whilst song-books do provide written arrangements, they are not really intended to be followed slavishly. Stuart Townend, who earns a living by writing such arrangements, explains how to use them, and ends by telling us to 'close the book and play the song from memory!'[4] This is obviously a completely new approach, which again does not come easily to many classically-trained musicians.

Worse than this, there is the phenomenon known as 'prophetic worship' which is basically where everyone makes it up as they go along, words, music, rhythm, the lot. They do so, of course, under the inspiration of the Spirit, so it's not as bad as it sounds, but they still need the skills to be able to do it. The Spirit may prompt me to get in the car to go and visit Mabel who is sick. But unless I have learnt to drive he can prompt all he likes but I simply won't be able to do it. So spiritual openness and sensitivity *and* a high degree of musical skill are required. You need a lot less of both if the most radical thing you will ever have to do is repeat the chorus.

7. Different Use of Musical Notation

As I have suggested, contemporary music is not meant to be played from dots on a sheet of manuscript paper. Ideally it is played entirely from memory, but two alternatives are *lead-lines* and *chord charts*. A lead-line is simply the melody of the song with its words, written out in musical notation, but with guitar chords underneath instead of another stave with a 'left-hand' part, so the players simply form the chords as appropriate to their instrument and to the style of the piece, rather as a baroque *continuo* player would create a part from the figuring on the score. A chord chart gives even less help than this, and simply tells which chords are to be played for how many beats. So the start of the *Jubilee Song* mentioned above would look like this:

---

4   S Townend, *Playing the Keyboard in Worship* (Eastbourne: Kingsway, 1993) p 23.

A /	/	/		/	/	/	/	D	/		/	/		/ / / /	

We have called on you | Lord and | you have heard us

where the vertical lines represent bar-lines and the slashes beats in the bar. This method of notation is clearly very easy to understand unless it involves unlearning decades of 'proper' music to be able to make sense of it.[5] And of course it gives you no help at all in knowing how the tune goes!

8. Different Skills and Skill Levels

It is clear from all this that much of what classical musicians have had drummed into them for years may not be just irrelevant: it may be positively harmful. On the other hand, if one begins without that background, the whole thing is notoriously easy. A guitarist with a vocabulary of only four chords can accompany many songs, a young child can switch on and off a digital drum machine at the right times, and a very unqualified pianist can, as long as they have learnt their Grade II arpeggios, put in a very effective accompaniment on a synthesizer patched to a 'strings' sound. Obviously the ideal is a high degree of musical skill combined with a flexible approach and ability, but you do not have to be much of a musician as long as you are musical, a quality sadly lacking in some formal training. Since one value of renewal music is its accessibility, it is very important that you do not have to be Grade VIII standard before you can begin.

Contextual Differences

So much for the musical style of worship songs. We will get a bit less technical here and look at them in the context of their use in worship. Not only are songs and hymns musically different, but they are designed to be used in completely different ways.

9. Different Purpose

This is one of the most fundamental but most rarely understood differences. Even *In Tune With Heaven*, which is otherwise very positive towards renewal music and musicians, is spoilt and loses credibility because it simply does not recognize this fact.[6] We said that one of the values of charismatic worship was intimacy with God. If that is so, it takes time. Charismatic worship has been described as a journey towards God. Like most journeys it begins from where we are now and ends where we want to be, so the songs

5 S Townend, *Op cit. passim* is excellent on the whole subject of learning to play from different notation and none.
6 *In Tune With Heaven The Report of the Archbishops' Commission on Church Music* (London: Church House/Hodder and Stoughton, 1992)

which take us on the journey need to be carefully chosen in order that there is a flow of both thought and mood. That is why most worship songs are used in the context of a 'worship slot,' an extended period of singing which may last for up to forty-five minutes in some churches. Hymns, on the other hand, are almost always stand-alone in design. The thought of singing one hymn after another for half an hour appeals to most people even less than singing one song after another!

10. Different Sequences

Since their purpose in worship is so different, it is easy to understand why they are designed to be used differently, and particularly in different sequences. When singing a hymn you begin at the beginning, go through until you reach the end, and then stop, unless the collection is not there yet. In extreme situations you might just go back and sing verse one again, and some more modern hymns do have a refrain after each verse (and maybe even twice at the end if you're really going) but basically there is a logical progression from A to Z. But worship songs are nowhere near as predictable. They are designed to be repeated, as a whole or just parts of them. There may be 'voice-overs' or instrumental sections inserted in the middle somewhere (the rhetoric of some churches explains that this is what the *selah* in the Psalms was). A single line may be repeated several times with a progressively different feel, getting louder and more triumphant, or dying away to a whisper. A chorus may be sung unaccompanied or with drums only, and so on. Flexibility is the watchword. To sing a song from start to finish as if it were a hymn is to miss the point. If worship is a journey into God's presence, the extended and varied use of a song makes that journey a ramble rather than a route-march. We may stop for a while to admire a view by letting the instruments play while we read through the words silently, or spend some time enjoying a small insight along the way by staying with one line, repeating it until it really sinks in.

11. Different Appeal

This leads on to another important difference which is often misunderstood (although the aforementioned 80/20 rule is needed especially here, and is perhaps nearer 60/40): hymns *tend* to impact the intellect, while songs *tend* to be aimed more at the emotions. That is why the purpose and sequence aspects we mentioned above are different. Hymns are there to teach or inform the mind, and therefore work in a logical progression. Songs on the other hand tend to touch the emotions, and as we all know emotions are not always logical. Other manifestations of this difference can be seen in the address of hymns and songs. Much more time is spent during charismatic worship in singing *to* God rather than to others *about* him.

Of course traditional hymns can and do touch our emotions. It is very difficult to sing *O love that wilt not let me go* without damp eyes. And of course some worship songs, such as Graham Kendrick's *Restore O Lord* and *Meekness and Majesty* are every bit as theologically heavyweight as anything Wesley wrote. But generally speaking charismatic worshippers tend to go into it for an emotional meeting with God. If their minds are informed as well, that is a pleasant by-product, but it is intimacy rather than information that they are after. One new Christian (a lady in her mid-forties) who joined our church, where we value and use both types, told me that she much preferred the 'songs on the wall' [the OHP] since they had 'so much more depth of meaning than the ones in the old hymn books,' an interesting reversal of the position of many critics of renewal music. I interpret this to mean that the worship she offered through songs touched her heart more deeply than did that through ancient hymns. Who is to say that this 'emotional' response is 'worse' than much of our dry, cerebral worship, offered week by week by Brits who are well-informed but terrified of their feelings?

12. Different Lifespan

Charismatic music is often criticized for its ephemeral nature, especially in the face of hymns which have lasted for several hundred years and are still going strong. Not only is this part of our transient modern culture, but it is deliberately so. Since many songs are designed primarily to work on the emotional level, they are of necessity short-lived, since there is no logical or theological content which will stand the test of time and outlive the emotional moment. It is therefore nonsense to publish worship songs in hymn books, since they will have died long before the hymns alongside them even begin to age.[7] Disposable song books, or even better, when the architecture permits, OHP acetates, are the most effective way of allowing the worshippers to see the words, and with the new copyright arrangements nobody need fear doing this illegally.[8] Songs are deliberately designed to allow worshippers to express the emotions which form the response to what God is doing *now* (here is that *immediacy* value), and will be very different in a few months' time. The songs which do stand the test of time are almost always those which look and feel most like hymns. This built-in disposability does not make songs 'worse' than hymns, any more than Pampers are worse than terry nappies. Only if you tried to reuse Pampers too many times would their value decrease!

I hope by this stage that you are beginning to be convinced that modern

---

7   Just look at the supplement to *Hymns for Today's Church* (London: Hodder and Stoughton, 1982). Hardly front-line stuff, is it?

8   For details of copyright for reproduction contact Christian Copyright Licensing at 26 Gildredge Rd, Eastbourne, East Sussex, BN21 4SA, (01323-417711).

church music is not modern traditional church music, but something with a whole different philosophy, structure and purpose behind it. Maybe you have recognized in what has been said so far some mistakes and difficulties you have been facing. So how can we begin to move into what we now know is a whole new world of worship? In the next section I will try to put up some signposts for beginners, both musicians and ministers, on this exploration.

3

Why Bother to Change?

Before beginning this exploration it is just worth pausing for a moment to decide whether we want or need to bother. Do we really want to wander into the charismatic woods, especially since it seems to require such fundamental changes in our whole style of worship, and the learning of a whole new set of skills? Why should we change? May I suggest six reasons?

1. Because It Fits Your Vision for Worship

This of course begs a few questions to do with whether you even have a vision for worship, whether you, or anyone else, knows whether or not you have one, and whether renewal music does fit it! But bearing in mind what we said about renewal music being nothing more than a symptom of a whole new spirituality, it simply will not do to bolt it on to an existing style where it really does not belong. As a member of three diocesan liturgical groups I have been involved in discussions with the hierarchy about the music for Diocesan events. I have argued long and hard against the approach which says 'We will stick *Majesty* in here to keep the charismatics happy!' because I believe it is nothing more than tokenism, since it does not look as though any attempt has been made to understand the real issues. So if you want your worship to be Spirit-filled and to seek immediacy, intimacy and involvement, you could well find modern music helpful. But if you do not, I should stick to Wesley. You would not find people laughing, crying or falling over in *his* services! (Or would you?)

2. Because It Works!

This too begs questions, but if you believe that churches are basically there to grow, you do need to take seriously the fact that the only churches consistently growing are those which make an effort to inculturate their music. The mushrooming of the 'new' (or 'house') churches over the past couple of decades, and their success not just at growth but also at keeping teenagers and attracting men as well as women is legendary,[9] and we have already noted how their contemporary worship style has influenced the established denominations considerably.[10] An interesting study from the Baptist denomination suggests that a range of musical styles, including material from a worship group rather than just a choir and an organ, will bias a church towards growth. And of course conversations with visitors back this up. Many outsiders who have seen our church at worship have commented to me that 'it was not at all like church!' Interestingly enough, I get similar comments from people who have been around in church for years just as they leave, but from non-Christians I take it to be a compliment, since I interpret it to mean 'it was not crashingly boring and irrelevant.' The music in particular is often singled out for praise.

3. Because It Can Include Younger Musicians More Easily

We have already noted that you don't need to be a highly qualified musician to have a crack at modern music, and many churches have found that some kind of a junior worship team can train up future instrumentalists and singers, as well as leading worship on some occasions, particularly in all-age worship. Youngsters have two important advantages over mature musicians: they listen to the stuff all the time on Radio 1; and they do not have years of classical training to unlearn. Our church music groups are helping to provide youngsters with a training in musicianship, improvisation, and so on, alongside their more formal music lessons.

4. Because It Can Provide Scope for Creativity

It can be highly rewarding for a church to make a song its own by treating it in a particular way or playing it in a style very different from the usual way. Whatever instrumental and vocal resources you have can be used to the full, and the song arranged to fit the available talent. This can breathe fresh life into worship, and can also relate the church effectively to the surrounding culture. Personally I love reggae, and in my previous parish we worked on a few songs, pushing them in this direction. The snag was that we were in the middle of a posh suburb with a large Asian population. Perhaps I was in the wrong job!

9 P Brierley, 'Christian' England (London: MARC, 1991) gives all the information about denominational growth patterns, and attempts some interpretation of the success of the New Churches (p 42ff).
10 P Beasley-Murray and A Wilkinson, Turning the Tide (London: Bible Society, 1981).

5. Because It Can Broaden Out a Monochrome Repertoire and Style

It is indeed variety, and not, as the music of some churches would suggest, *Venite*, which is the spice of life, adding interest and excitement to an otherwise bland diet. If we are to do justice to the creator God who enables us to share in his creativity, we really do need to explore ways in which that creativity can be brought into our worship. Let me repeat what I said earlier: it is not that renewal music is better than traditional music. But renewal music *and* traditional music, mixed together and used appropriately, is better than either alone. Also, it needs to be said that this booklet has made no mention of other strands currently available, from Taizé to Iona via NOS, which can each add to the richness of a church's worship if appropriately used.

6. Because 'In Tune with Heaven' Recommends It

This is the clincher. Renewal music does get a fairly good press throughout the book, in spite of the apparent failure of the Commission really to understand it, and several of the recommendations on pages 252ff suggest that it would do us all good at least to explore renewal music. That settles it, really, doesn't it? What choice do we have?

4
How Do I Begin?

So it might be right for you to begin exploring the use of modern renewal worship. How might you go about it? This next section will give you some ideas. I want to make it as practical as possible, and I have aimed it at musicians rather than at ministers, although a wise minister will obviously want to understand all he or she can about what the musicians are trying to do. So read this first yourself, and then if you are not musical, pass it to someone who is, with the encouragement from you to begin having a go. I gladly acknowledge right from the start my debt to Stuart Townend who through his writing and workshops has helped so many people begin this journey. Much of the material in this section is borrowed from Stuart, and his book cannot be recommended highly enough.[11] Here are eight suggestions to get you going.

1. Cultivate Wonder and Respect
I hope you have realized by now that you may be stepping into a whole new world if you have only ever been classically trained and used traditional worship music. Suddenly things are different: it is like entering a foreign land. Do so with awe. Do not be like a holidaymaker in Spain who spends his whole time moaning because the beer is warm and the chips greasy and the place is full of foreigners and everything back in England is much better. Perhaps he should have stayed in at home if he feels like that. Go instead as a pilgrim. Revel in the new things to be learned and experienced from this strange culture, know what you do not know, be discerning about what you swallow, and return enriched, bringing to your church's worship new insights and ways of doing things.

2. Get a Good Guide
There are all sorts of resources designed to help people like you. Training events abound, skilled worship musicians are only too glad to teach others, and you can visit other churches from time to time to see how they handle their music. Go to your local Christian book shop, buy a copy of one of the worship magazines such as *Deo*, and read the advertisements for courses you can sign up for. You do not have to travel alone!

---

11 *Op cit.*

3. Brush Up Your Keyboard Harmony

You probably did not realize it at the time, but the most important thing you learnt in those piano lessons before you stopped at Grade III was your arpeggios. If you know them, you can play worship keyboards, and if you understand how they work you can transfer easily onto the guitar or bass. If you have done music theory and harmony to a higher level than that, you will have a good working knowledge of how chords function. If you have not, you will need to learn, so find someone who can teach you. Learn what tonics and dominants are, what V7d means, what a diminished chord is, how guitar chords relate to classical figuring, and you are away. Stuart's book can help tremendously here, but a personal guide will be even better. Is there someone you know doing 'A' level music? They will help, and it may do them good too!

4. Begin to Understand the Technology

This is complicated, and you don't need to know it all, but a basic knowledge of *synthesis*, *sampling* and *MIDI* can be tremendously enriching to a church's worship musicians. I will attempt a brief noddy-guide in the next few paragraphs.

There are basically two ways of producing music electronically. The first is *synthesis*, and this was popular in the sixties and seventies. You are probably aware that you can 'see' electronically what music looks like on an oscilloscope. The purest sound is made by what is called a 'sine-wave.' A picture of it would look something like this:

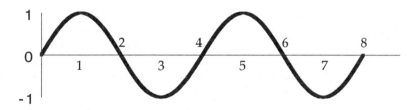

This would sound like a very pure flute. The height of the curves would vary with the volume of the sound, and the pitch of the note with their 'wavelength,' or the time it takes the line to go from zero to plus to zero to minus to zero again. This is a *cycle*, and musical wavelength is measured in cycles per second. At standard *concert pitch* the A above middle C does this 440 times per second. A faster speed would produce a higher note, a slower speed a lower one.

So why does a flute playing A sound different from a violin playing the same note? Because of *harmonics* and *overtones*. Rather than the pure curve above, each instrument has a unique blend of other curves going on around it, which makes the sound different from the pure sine-wave tone and different from any other instrument.

Synthesis is what the name suggests: the building up of sounds from their basic components by adding waves or changing them. A basic synthesizer would have four oscillators, each of which produces a sound which can be fiddled around with in various ways. Obviously it is fairly difficult to synthesize accurate sounds in this way: a basic synthesizer would never really sound convincingly like a clarinet or guitar, but it would be good at weird sounds which normal instruments cannot do. Much rock and pop music of the 60s and 70s explored synthesis in this way.

But now the trend is to move to a much more accurate creation of authentic sounds through *digital sampling*. Think back to our sine-wave above. The way it is drawn is an *analogue* style, in other words the diagram does represent pictorially something approximating to reality, or analogous to it. But it would be possible to represent the same facts in another way. Rather than drawing the graph pictorially, we could simply give a set of co-ordinates. At its simplest this could be $(0,0)(1,+1)(2,0)(3,-1)(4,0)$, but clearly the thinner slices along the horizontal axis you take, the more accurate the curve. Now imagine doing this for a complex curve full of harmonics, representing, say, the sound of a saxophone. By playing A on a real sax into a machine called a sampler, you can store the sound digitally, simply as a set of numbers.

This has two important advantages. Firstly, numbers do not decay. A sound stored on tape or record can be lost or distorted due to physical wear and tear on the medium. But a number three is always a number three. So much better and longer-lasting reproduction is possible. That is how CDs work. But secondly, and more significantly for our discussion, you can alter numbers mathematically if you want to. So a sampler can decide which numbers relate to a note's pitch, and alter them to give higher and lower pitches. One 'A' played into a sampler by the sax will enable it to reproduce eight octaves' worth of sax sounds. Similarly you can record a piece digitally and alter the tempo numbers but not the pitch numbers. A tape recording would alter both together, giving a kind of 'worship-with-the-chipmunks' sound, but with sampling you can slow down or speed up a recording for practice purposes. Similarly transposition is available at the press of a button, as the sampler alters the pitch but not the speed. And different tonal qualities can be achieved by tweaking some of the numbers relating to harmonics.

MIDI stands for 'musical instrument digital interface,' and it is an internationally-recognized way of allowing different instruments to control each other. It is possible to connect up several different instruments to one keyboard, and to play them all at the same time, using the volume controls of each to mix and blend the sound. And instruments other than keyboards can be used. A MIDI guitar can be used to control a sampler which has pipe organ sounds programmed into it, and you can even get digital wind instruments which you blow and finger like a clarinet but which can produce whatever sounds your keyboard or sound module has in it. Digital drums are also available, which can be hit with sticks or played on preset rhythms simply by pressing buttons.

What this means is that there is almost unlimited versatility available for a fraction of the cost of even the most basic church organ (in fact many church organs are now switching to digital sound). Keyboard players are in great demand, because they can do the job of just about anyone else. If a song really cries out for a flute, and you haven't got a real one, just press the flute button and off you go. Many worship groups regularly use first and second keyboards. The first, set to a piano or electric piano sound, will keep the rhythm and harmony going, whilst the second can weave other instrumental sounds in and out, and can even provide drums if necessary.

So if you are a classically-trained organist you do not need a physics degree to play renewal music, but a basic awareness of what is going on technologically will help you get the most out of the group and its hardware.

5. Move from a Visual to an Aural Recognition of Music

Increasing numbers of youngsters (and adults) are learning to play musical instruments by the 'Suzuki Method,' which is based around hearing a tune and reproducing it before ever seeing it written on manuscript paper, but it is probably true to say that the vast majority of musicians have been taught to *see* music and then play it rather than to *hear* it and play it. That's why many players are completely at sea if you do take their books away. Since modern church music is much more based around improvisation and playing by ear, it is important to make the switch from visual to aural learning. This is, of course, a part of the traditional music curriculum, with aural tests included in the Grade exams, but only a small part, and one with which many struggle. This needs developing, and that can happen by listening carefully to music, analysing what chords sound like in relation to each other, knowing what likely sequences will probably come up, and so on. Begin with simple songs, like *Jesus we enthrone you*, and try to guess, and then to work out on your keyboard or guitar, what you think the chords might be. Listen especially to the bass line (adjusting your stereo as necessary), and you will get a good clue as to where the chords are going. Try also to work out what the chords might be in a range of different keys, and think of the harmony in relative rather than absolute terms (if you have been trained in Roman numeral notation this will help, as will a familiarity with terms such as *dominant*, *submediant*, and so on).

If this sounds complicated and technical, it is! But as with all endeavours, it gets easier with practice, and it can be liberating in worship once mastered.

6. Mess Around When No-one is Listening

If practice is important, experimentation is even more so. Buy a copy of Stuart's book, work through the exercises he provides, and fiddle around making up chords and sounds as they appeal to you. 'If it feels good, do it!' may not be appropriate when it comes to morality, but here it is the name of the game. If your keyboard has a headphone socket you need not let anyone else be a party to your experimentation. If not, just wait until they have gone out. Practice is no longer about learning what the book says; it is much more to do with feel. What sounds as if it adds to the overall impression of a song? Go with what is helpful, and go back to the keyboard with what is not.

7. Listen Analytically to Recordings

There is so much modern music now available on tape or CD that it is possible to listen to the way in which the composer thinks the music should go. So listen hard and work out what arrangements he or she uses, what fancy chords have been put in, and so on. You may feel that you could arrange the music even more effectively, or you may have a different set of instruments with which to work, but understanding from a recording will at least give you a base from which to start.

8. Cultivate Rhythmic Playing

Of course a whole variety of styles will be appropriate for worship musicians, but we have argued that rhythm is the commodity in greatest demand nowadays. A good exercise is to take a piece such as Bach's *Prelude No 1 in C* (from the *48*, Book I), and experiment with playing it in block chords, rather than arpeggios, to different rhythms. If you can get hold of a drum machine, try the piece to a variety of rhythms, such as Latin, heavy metal, reggae, rap and so on. Do not worry too much about Bach's subterranean revolutions— I am sure he would understand. Then try the same with worship songs which are familiar to you, and see what works and what is disastrous.

9. Read 'Living Liturgy'

A personal plug to end with, if I may be so bold. My book gives much more detail about the use of music (and words) in renewal worship, and is particularly (although not exclusively) applicable to an Anglican setting.[12] There are practical tips for both clergy and musicians, and people have been kind enough to tell me that it has helped them. I hope it might help you too!

---

12 J Leach, *Living Liturgy* (Eastbourne: Kingsway, 1997)